DEEP SEA FISHERMAN

BY NICK GORDON

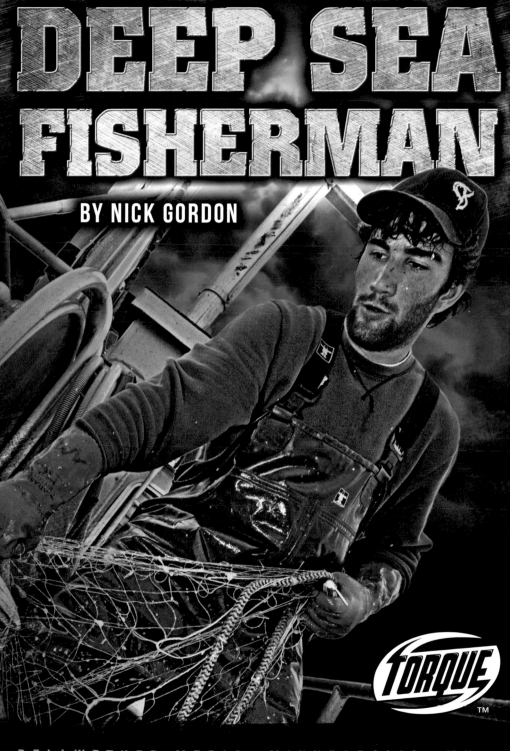

BELLWETHER MEDIA · MINNEAPOLIS, MN

Are you ready to take it to the extreme?
Torque books thrust you into the action-packed world
of sports, vehicles, mystery, and adventure. These books
may include dirt, smoke, fire, and dangerous stunts.
WARNING: read at your own risk.

Library of Congress Cataloging-in-Publication Data

Gordon, Nick.
Deep sea fisherman / by Nick Gordon.
    p. cm. -- (Torque: Dangerous jobs)
Includes bibliographical references and index.
 Summary: "Engaging images accompany information about deep sea fishermen. The combination of
high-interest subject matter and light text is intended for students in grades 3 through 7"--Provided by
publisher.
 ISBN 978-1-60014-779-1 (hbk. : alk. paper)
 1. Fishers--Juvenile literature. 2. Big game fishing--Juvenile literature. 3. Hazardous occupations--
Juvenile literature. I. Title.
 HD8039.F65G67 2013
 639.2023--dc23

                          2012004408

This edition first published in 2013 by Bellwether Media, Inc.

Printed in the United States of America, North Mankato, MN.

TABLE OF CONTENTS

CHAPTER 1

MAN OVERBOARD!

A cold wind blasts across the Bering Sea. A small crab fishing boat is tossed back and forth by the rough water. Brave fishermen cling to the boat's rails. Suddenly, a **rogue wave** slams into the boat. One of the fishermen is swept overboard!

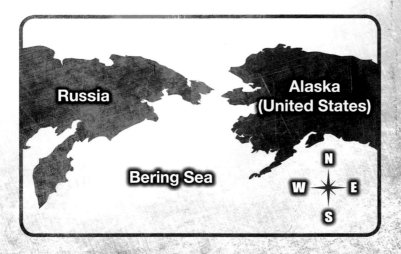

Russia

Alaska
(United States)

Bering Sea

N
W E
S

Deep Sea Death Toll

In the United States, between 40 and 50 deep sea fishermen die on the job each year.

The other fishermen rush to rescue the man. He will not survive long in the freezing water. They throw him a rescue line, but the wind sends it off course. A second throw also misses. The man is getting farther and farther from the boat. One final throw lands within his reach. The man grabs hold and the others pull him to safety.

7

CHAPTER 2

DEEP SEA FISHERMEN

Deep sea fishermen know their job is one of the most dangerous in the world. They battle harsh seas to catch crabs, salmon, and other seafood. They often work 15 hours or more every day for weeks at a time.

Danger Pays

Crab fishermen can earn as much as $50,000 during a successful trip to sea. Some of these trips last less than a week.

Deep sea fishermen train on the job. New fishermen are called **greenhorns**. They do difficult, dirty work on the **deck**. Greenhorns slice and prepare the slimy **bait**. They also chop ice off the boat's rails and deck.

Greenhorns work to become **deckhands**. Deckhands operate the machines that lower and raise nets, lines, and **crab pots**. They sort and clean catches and repair equipment. Sometimes they steer the boat. Deckhands take orders from the **captain**.

CHAPTER 3
DANGER!

Deep sea fishermen work in **unpredictable** conditions. Calm breezes and small waves can quickly turn into massive storms. Heavy rain and icy winds often batter fishermen and their boats. Rogue waves can throw crew members overboard. Boats can sink if they take on too much water.

Top Causes of Death

1. Sinking boat
2. Falling overboard
3. Onboard injury

Most fishing boats have many ropes and lines. Fishermen can get caught in these. A rope or line that quickly tightens can break or **sever** an arm or leg. It can also pull a fisherman overboard into ice-cold water. Many fishermen who fall in drown or die from **hypothermia**.

Fishermen take steps to stay safe. Many wear **flotation devices** in case they fall overboard. Good captains make sure their boats are not carrying too much weight. They also do regular **inspections** to make sure nothing is wrong with their boats.

The hours are long and the work is hard. The excitement and money keep deep sea fishermen heading back for more. The possibility of death does not stop them from battling the merciless sea.

Tragedy on the Job

On April 2, 2001, the *Arctic Rose* sank in the Bering Sea. All 15 members of the crew died. When it sank, winds were reported to be gusting at about 52 miles (83 kilometers) per hour. Waves rose up to 24 feet (7 meters).

Glossary

bait—pieces of fish used to lure ocean animals to nets, lines, and traps

captain—a fisherman who owns and operates a boat; the captain manages the crew and decides where to fish.

crab pots—cages used to capture crabs; fishermen put bait in crab pots and then lower them into the water.

deck—the main outside area of a boat; fishermen do most of their work on the deck.

deckhands—fishermen with some experience; deckhands operate machines and fix nets and lines.

flotation devices—objects or vests used to help people stay afloat

greenhorns—deep sea fishermen in training; greenhorns do difficult, dirty work.

hypothermia—a condition in which a person's body temperature is very low; people with hypothermia are at risk of dying.

inspections—careful safety examinations; captains inspect their boats to make sure they are fit to head out to sea.

rogue wave—a giant wave; rogue waves often surprise crews because they seem to come out of nowhere.

sever—to cut off

unpredictable—having behavior that is hard or impossible to guess

To Learn More

AT THE LIBRARY

Jenkins, Steve. *Down, Down, Down: A Journey to the Bottom of the Sea*. Boston, Mass.: Houghton Mifflin Harcourt, 2009.

Johnson, Jinny. *Deep Sea Life*. Mankato, Minn.: Smart Apple Media, 2012.

Thomas, William. *Deep Sea Fishing*. New York, N.Y.: Marshall Cavendish Benchmark, 2010.

ON THE WEB

Learning more about deep sea fishermen is as easy as 1, 2, 3.

1. Go to www.factsurfer.com.

2. Enter "deep sea fishermen" into the search box.

3. Click the "Surf" button and you will see a list of related Web sites.

With factsurfer.com, finding more information is just a click away.

Index